UNLOCKING INSTANT CASH

UNLOCKING INSTANT CASH

Strategies for Financial Success in the Digital Age

JIM STEPHENS

ECONO Publishing Company

CONTENTS

Every effort has been made by the publisher to ensure the precision and comprehensiveness of this report. Nevertheless, it is critical to specify that owing to the dynamic nature of the Internet, they do not provide any assurance or representation regarding the accuracy of the contents.

Notwithstanding every reasonable endeavor to authenticate the data presented in this publication, the publisher disclaims any liability for inaccuracies, omissions, or any alternative understanding of the subject matter. Any inadvertent slights directed at particular individuals, groups, or institutions are merely perceived.

Like life itself, practical advice books do not provide any assurance of financial gain. Readers are advised to exercise their own discernment with respect to their specific situations and to take appropriate action in response.

It is imperative to underscore that this literary work should not be regarded as a substitute for legal, business, accountancy, or financial counsel. It is recommended that all readers retain the expertise of seasoned professionals in the domains of law, commerce, finance, and accounting.

Introduction

This book outlines a selection of the most efficient strategies for generating income online, guaranteeing immediate funds within a minimal timeframe. Surely no additional introductions are required? So, raise your feet, relax, and begin reading.

Instant Funds

A multitude of websites and eBooks assert that engaging in online work can yield thousands of dollars per day, contingent upon the purchase of their eBooks, which purport to contain a miraculous formula, for approximately $49.99. To what extent is this statement accurate? Sadly, a significant number of these assurances prove to be fraudulent schemes that make hollow assurances after stealing your hard-earned cash. Those who are duped into such schemes bear responsibility for their own actions.

Actually, achieving wealth online does not require any shortcuts. It reflects practical situations in which earning daily sustenance requires diligence and well-considered endeavors.

Comparable to the real world, achieving success online necessitates the consistent application of acquired skills and the continuous development of new ones. Similar to conventional employment, generating a livelihood online requires a disciplined commitment of a specific number of hours per day. Success in the online realm is attained by those who have a comprehensive understanding of their respective fields, avoid fraudulent schemes, and employ diligence and expertise.

The forthcoming chapters will explore diverse methods by which one can generate income online in exchange for one hour of dedicated effort. Already, millions of people across the globe are working from the convenience of their own residences in these online projects. You are granted the autonomy to establish your own schedule, accept payments via international payment systems such as PayPal, or even by cheque denominated in your domestic currency.

The internet has provided access to an abundance of information in the hyper-connected world of today. Despite lacking formal degrees and training, one can acquire knowledge rapidly through sheer determination. Leverage your social circle of acquaintances, English proficiency, and internet navigation skills to advance your abilities. You will be able to begin earning in at least a portion of the areas covered in the following chapters in due course.

CHAPTER 3

Google AdSense is utilized.

Google's AdSense is among the most extensively utilized advertising programs on the web. Presently, "Ads by Google" are present on virtually every website, often in strategic locations such as the page's left, right, bottom, or even center. With each view on such an advertisement, the advertiser pays a nominal fee to the webmaster via Google AdSense. Consisting of billions of page views, AdSense generates millions of dollars in daily revenue for ads, making it the most popular pay-per-click (PPC) program in the world.

Potential click-through compensation ranges from a few cents to twenty or more dollars. Producing niche content that is pertinent to particular specialized keywords can result in substantial financial gains. Nevertheless, establishing a website featuring only these lucrative keywords and deploying AdSense advertisements is inadequate. For a website to attract adequate traffic and authentic ad views, it must provide the reader with valuable information. Participating in click fraud activities, including encouraging peers to click on one's own advertisements or doing so themselves, may result in the immediate removal of those advertisements from one's webpage by AdSense.

As a result, it is recommended that you create a website or blog centered around a topic that both captivates your interest and has the potential to generate revenue for you as an advertiser, provided that it is commercially viable. AdSense algorithms conduct daily page scans in order to insert advertisements that are pertinent to the content of your webpages.

Blogger.com simplifies the process of creating a blog to three stages. After that, fully engage in your selected field by producing unique material that integrates pertinent keywords. Encourage your peers to forward your blog's link in order to increase traffic. Share the hyperlink on the websites of your acquaintances and engage in discussions forums that are pertinent to the subject matter.

Sitemeter.com is an example of a traffic monitoring website that can be used to track daily page views and visits. The Dashboard of your AdSense account will offer comprehensive information regarding the click volume and your revenues. The aforementioned information can be found on the account page. Additionally, AdSense provides insightful guidance on how to advertise placements for maximum revenue. Therefore, enhance your blog or website with the assistance of Google AdSense!

CHAPTER 4

Turk Mechanically

Have you ever pondered ways to supplement your income during your free time? Mechanical Turk provides precisely that.

Mturk.com, an online marketing behemoth owned by Amazon, features thousands of HITs (Human Intelligence Tasks) on its pages. The compensation for accomplishing these varyingly difficult duties ranges from a few cents to tens of dollars. Participating in a forum, composing a few paragraphs on a given subject, or undertaking a survey are all examples of simpler assignments. Proficiency in greater intricacy may be necessary for endeavors such as web design, comprehensive report composition, or market research. Additionally, there are audio transcription tasks where you can earn a few dollars by converting audio clips of five to ten minutes in length to text.

Mturk functions as an exceptional platform for preparing oneself for increasingly specialized online employment opportunities. By honing your writing abilities and gaining self-assurance through the composition of 100- to 200-word articles, you can gradually progress towards undertaking more substantial freelance writing projects on platforms such as ODesk, Elance, and GetAFreelancer, which will be covered in subsequent chapters.

Successfully mastering audio transcription and attaining a respectable level of speed and accuracy will enable you to eventually transition into the lucrative fields of legal or medical transcription on a full-time basis. Although specialized training may be required in these domains, the straightforward duties in Mechanical Turk serve as a solid foundation.

An assessment of your work is conducted and remuneration is deposited into your Mturk account within a few hours to days. It is crucial to remain vigilant for lucrative opportunities, such as completing a brief survey for a few dollars or composing a 400-word article on Icelandic tourism for three dollars. It is a prevalent practice among journalists and media writers today to conduct a brief online search in order to generate a credible and factual presentation, notwithstanding one's lack of familiarity with the subject matter.

In certain countries, payments are processed through bank transfers, cheques denominated in the local currency, or through the use of funds in the account to purchase items from Amazon.com.

It is an excellent method to begin thousands of simple duties and prepare for greater opportunities in the future. A spare hour should not be wasted. Today, become a Turker. Additionally, remember to visit a reputable Turker forum for the most recent developments and an abundance of helpful advice.

CHAPTER 5

Article Composition

Do you consider writing your passion? Has it ever been your ambition to write a best-selling book? Many accomplished novelists, in fact, maintained a day job as well. A day job that pays a respectable salary and allows you to continue writing in your field of interest will give you more time to complete your blockbuster novel.

Individuals who possess a proficient command of the English language are capable of composing a few paragraphs of novel material. Even more straightforward is to read an article and rewrite it. The aforementioned statement adequately encapsulates the job description of a highly profitable online position at present.

As tens of thousands of fresh websites are launched each hour, administrators are perpetually in search of new content for their sites. Some websites are created through the process of transforming the same content into numerous articles. The majority of article purchasers pay between one and two dollars to rewrite a 300-500 word article. This may be a fifteen- to thirty-minute task, contingent upon your typing speed and language proficiency.

It is essential to maintain originality; write the content in your own terms, as the majority of buyers employ copy-detection software such as Copyscape and Plagium to detect plagiarism. Copyscape will identify any instances of copying and pasting from external websites; doing so could result in the rejection of your assignment and adverse feedback from the buyer.

Proofread your article thoroughly before submitting it, using tools such as SpellCheck if you use Microsoft Word. While lacking expertise in a specific subject matter, dedicating a portion of your time to peruse pertinent online sources may furnish you with sufficient material to compose a 500-word article.

Such is the appeal of online freelance writing. Engaging in daily article research and writing substantially broadens one's general knowledge. Engaging in this practice will not only hone your inventive writing abilities but also lay the foundation for a future blockbuster novel.

Investigate sites such as Getafreelancer.com, Elance.com, and Odesk.com, and register with the one that best meets your needs. Payment facilitation is achieved via PayPal as well as other globally recognized systems.

CHAPTER 6

An instruct

Utilizing an exceptional talent is one of the most gratifying methods of earning money online.

Could you instruct an audience on a particular language or show them how to unclog a drain? Merely procure a digital camera, document yourself demonstrating your proficiency, and publish the video to YouTube. Post the link to pertinent forums and distribute it to your social circle. Then, develop a straightforward specialized website with additional instructional videos. Grant viewers exclusive access in exchange for a nominal payment made through PayPal or credit card. It is recommended that you incorporate a hyperlink to this website into your complimentary YouTube videos.

You can begin generating revenue as your website gains more subscribers as your videos amass thousands of views. Additionally, you can publish and sell eBooks on your website that are tailored to your particular subject.

Provide a substantial number of pertinent hyperlinks to

analogous websites that your members may find useful. Although it may appear paradoxical, subscribers value this candor and support, which in turn strengthens their allegiance.

This strategy permits you to pursue your passions while receiving compensation from the world. It is effortless to establish a free webpage or blog (via platforms such as Blogger.com), track website traffic (via tools like Sitemeter.com), or generate electronic books (via eBook Pro) by utilizing the multitude of tools that are readily accessible on the internet.

The benefit of remote work is the ability to utilize one's residence's facilities, utilities, and fixtures without incurring additional expenses for a physical store. Creating a small studio for instructing artistic abilities such as sculpting, candlemaking, or even making simple handcrafted cards is possible. Already, tens of thousands of YouTube videos span topics such as dance and music.

Determine your niche and pursue it. It may take some time to build a successful business, but if you provide something distinctive, it can go viral on YouTube, allowing you to profit from your achievements.

CHAPTER 7

Electronic books

During its initial surge in prominence, the internet was predominantly perceived as a conduit for communication and information exchange. The importance of the information component was substantial, as individuals now possessed an exceptional means of locating the information they required at any time. Presently, this perception of the internet endures, and shrewd individuals are exploiting it in a multitude of methods.

One notable pathway involves the production and distribution of electronic books (eBooks). eBooks, which stand for electronic books, are subject-specific informational publications. They comprise a portion of the subject matter and are typically (though not always) self-help guides, which are the most popular and profitable.

The idea is uncomplicated: identify a subject that is in high demand for information and produce an eBook pertaining to it. Write in a straightforward, basic style that a layperson can comprehend. Once your eBook is complete, promote it via multiple online channels, including social networking sites, affiliate marketing, the creation of a webpage and sales page, and affiliate marketing. As the popularity of your eBook increases, so will the level of interest from potential buyers.

There are primarily two methods for monetizing eBooks. You can utilize them as an instrument to sell a larger product or sell them separately for profit. Alternatively, you might not even be permitted to charge for your eBook. On the internet, the practice of providing valuable content for free is widespread and encourages interested parties to purchase more comprehensive products.

Therefore, what could you publish an eBook on? Consider anything that you are aware of that others may find useful. It may pertain to the most efficient method for cleaning glass windows or locating mortgage providers for a newly constructed residence. The crucial element is to earn money by instructing.

CHAPTER 8

The Affiliate Sector

On the internet, affiliate marketing is an extremely prevalent concept. Essentially, it is a revenue-generating strategy in which you endorse an external product on your website or blog in exchange for linking to the advertiser's site. The individuals you refer are known as "traffic," and they are typically compensated via a pay-per-click (PPC) model, comparable to Google AdSense. You are compensated for every click that you successfully direct to the advertiser's website link. PPL (payment per lead) and PPS (payment per transaction) are two additional payment models.

Presented here is a technique that can generate income for you even during your sleep. After the advertisement has been configured and promotional campaigns have been executed, individuals will be directed to the advertiser's website in an automated fashion, resulting in the generation of revenue. Consistently earned without further exertion, this form of funds is referred to as passive income or residual income.

Your principal objective is to increase the visibility of the affiliate links on your website or blog, thereby motivating a greater number of individuals to click through them. Your revenue is proportional in direct ratio to the quantity of individuals you successfully refer. The visibility of your website can be increased through the implementation of several strategies discussed in this article, including blogging, article submission and writing, and so forth.

A significant factor contributing to the current surge in popularity of affiliate marketing is the extended payment structure. If everything is properly organized, funds will continue to flow in. In contrast to alternative methods, payments continue to accrue notwithstanding the continuous exertion. Upon diligent planning and execution for a few months, you may observe tens of thousands of dollars deposited into your account on a monthly basis.

Nonetheless, it is an instant cash method as the funds begin to flow virtually instantaneously, usually within the initial week.

CHAPTER 9

Exploration of Website Spinning

This is a popular method of obtaining income instantly. It affords the opportunity for self-expression, exerts minimal effort, and has the potential to yield substantial financial gains. Nonetheless, some technical expertise is required to get started. However, a dearth of technical expertise should not deter you; you can always outsource the handling of any aspects with which you are uneasy.

Therefore, what is website rotation exactly? It is the process by which individuals construct and resell websites for a financial gain. The principal objective of developing the website is to subsequently sell it, and a skillfully constructed website offers significant profit potential. The following are several crucial factors that website spinners consider:

◇ Their ability to select exceptional domain names is a substantial contributor to their success. It is essential to ensure that domain names are optimized for search engines and have a high recall value.

They develop succinct websites. These websites are deliberately designed to be brief in order to promote rapid turnover. A website intended for browsing generally comprises a maximum of ten pages.

◈ The websites are replete with academically valuable content. Once more, the content is extensively optimized for search engines (SEO), encompassing a multitude of frequently queries keywords.

◈ The website's design and overall appearance are relatively uncomplicated. This feature enables the purchaser to effortlessly personalize the website to suit their own tastes.

The sale proceeds are contingent on the website's quality. You should anticipate a minimum of $50 for a ten-page website, which is a reasonable starting point. A website that has achieved some level of popularity on Google may be able to be sold for a significantly higher price. The selling process typically occurs on forums, with the Digital Point Forums serving as a prominent platform for this purpose.

CHAPTER 10

Technical Provisions

Utilizing any type of technical expertise to generate income on the internet is possible. For instance, individuals with expertise in website design may be able to obtain online opportunities to create websites for others. Whether $10 to $100 per page is acceptable to a client depends on a variety of factors, including the website's budget, the intricacy of the webpage, your expertise, and reputation.

Designing websites is merely one instance of a technically oriented service that can be offered profitably. There are numerous others in comparable fields, including graphic design, which is also an exceptionally lucrative domain. For example, creating a logo for a business could generate hundreds of shekels. Conversely, providing a client with animation or video services expands the scope of potential outcomes significantly.

Where then might one locate such opportunities? Among the finest locations are numerous freelance job boards. The following are some examples:

oDesk → ScriptLance → GetAFreelancer → Guru → ELance

You secure employment on these websites via a bidding system. Service-seeking parties publish their needs, and you compete for these opportunities through bids. The delivery schedule for the project is specified in your proposal; therefore, submitting samples may increase your chances of success. Samples and proposals are evaluated by purchasers prior to selecting the most qualified candidates.

Moreover, one can locate potential consumers through social networking sites. Engaging with groups on social media platforms such as Twitter and Facebook can serve as a productive means of establishing connections with like-minded individuals, potentially resulting in lucrative business prospects. It is essential to note, however, that these platforms do not function as job boards and should not be your primary resource for locating online employment.

CHAPTER 11

A Few Points to Bear in Mind

It is important to note that any income generated remotely via the internet is subject to taxation, and you bear the responsibility of remitting your own taxes. Although only a minority of clients may require your services in the field of taxation, those who do are probably interested in a lasting partnership. Nevertheless, with regard to immediate cash methods, taxation is your responsibility.

It is essential to establish an online banking account. The foremost online banking platform is PayPal (http://www.paypal.com/), with Moneybookers (http://www.moneybookers.com/) following suit. Numerous online employment platforms additionally function as payment distributors, from which you may procure checks directly.

Distractions can be detrimental when earning for oneself; therefore, maintain concentration. When engaging in online labor via freelance websites, an evaluation system is implemented. Your future prospects may be jeopardized by a single negative rating, since clients form opinions about you according to your rating.

Ongoing education is vital. Those who acquire the most knowledge typically earn the most on the internet. On an almost daily basis, novel techniques and strategies emerge, and remaining well-informed can significantly improve one's prospects. Rapidly becoming a highly competitive environment, it is crucial to maintain a competitive edge in the online realm.

It is important not to become disheartened if initial earnings are inadequate. The majority of immediate cash strategies may initially generate modest returns, but as you gain experience, you can demand greater returns. Additionally, your opportunities and earnings increase as you gain ratings. Collect ratings similarly to how you would experience for your portfolio.

Embark on an exploration of the digital realm. You have access to a multitude of prospects that allow you to exhibit your aptitudes and assess your financial capabilities.

To conclude,

There exists a plethora of strategies that offer immediate cash, and this eBook elucidates the most optimal ones. By effectively implementing these strategies, you will never again encounter difficulties in procuring the meager amounts required to pay your expenses.

You may even discover that you have amassed the most wealth in your personal network. This can be accomplished with sufficient time, effort, and knowledge.

Best wishes for the remainder of your voyage!